HOUSE OF CARDS

CHARLES BOYLE

House of Cards

CARCANET NEW PRESS / MANCHESTER

Acknowledgements are due to the editors of *PN Review, London Magazine, The Times Literary Supplement, The New Statesman* and *Encounter* in which some of these poems first appeared; and also to the Radio 3 'Poetry Now' programme.

First published in 1982 by
Carcanet New Press Ltd
330-332 Corn Exchange Buildings
Manchester M4 3BG

The publisher acknowledges the financial assistance of the Arts Council of Great Britain.

Printed in Britain by Short Run Press Ltd., Exeter

CONTENTS

6

And I began to understand what the obligatory nature of colour is—the excitement of sky-blue and orange football shirts—and that colour is nothing other than a sense of the start of a race, a sense tinged by distance and locked into its size.

Mandelstam, *Journey to Armenia*, trans. Clarence Brown.

THE SCHOOL ATLAS

The geography teacher's smug monotone
Is spliced with gunshots—a Messerschmitt 109
Nose-dives into the North Sea, its pilot
Still dangling beneath his parachute.

Other days were calmer, I'd doodle
Sea-monsters, a Mexican bandit with bandoliers,
Or stare through the window at passing clouds
Like continents unravelling . . .

I doubt the teacher himself, replaying
The same set syllabus year by year, ever hoped
For more. Boring us with statistics,
He made us look between the lines

Into woodland or open fields where lovers
Hide, a tramp falls asleep in the warmth
Of a ditch, the surviving generations
Lay out their baskets for a Sunday picnic.

Also those anonymous places we dreamed
Our future in, named now and trapped in the web
With our precise addresses, as real
And inescapable as my random Osmiroid inkblots.

A STUDY OF DOORS

How doors admit strangers

And how they are used
For instance, as frames for parting shots,
To camouflage retreats, or slammed in anger
Later regretted

For privacy, and to escape from this

How some
Remain closed, preserving things in their places,
While others are always open—come, go,
My house is yours—signalling trust
In an ideal, generous, continuously
Evolving world . . .

I do not know yet which is better.
Only one thing I have learned,
One cannot pass through the same door twice:
I came late, I had already gone

And you were out or maybe sleeping.
I waited some time on the cool steps.

DĒJĀ VU

I open the door (see the door opened
By no one at all, then look down and see
A child come out) and come out
Into the early light.

Along the sea-front
The night-shift workers are cycling home
With tired legs. Or a gull takes off
From the old fire-station roof.

I enter this town as you would
A novel, bravely attempting
The more difficult words
And taking for real what is not.

But the old men muttering
Outside the pub, by the wall with TROOPS OUT
Scrawled above them, I have seen them before
In the forest at night.

WET SPRING NIGHT

A room stripped bare, then painted white
On brilliant white till it sang
Like champagne of all possible space . . .

That night glistens
With headlights, tail-lights, reds
And panic yellows: I saw shadows

At noon, a mute third chair
At our table for two, the lines were crossed
Whenever we tried to phone out.

Three workmen sitting there
Were rolling cigarettes and drinking tea,
They beckoned me in through the glass.

INTERIOR

Not wholly enclosed, for already a door
Opens or a wall is missing
For you to see in. Excuse the mess

I say, I was just about—but you
Take it as found, everything muddled,
Unfinished, and lying about at odd angles

To myself: here the open books
Contradicting each other, there the laughing
Plants and bottles and a lonely glove

That mourns its fellow, lost in the spaces
I call it from. The echoes returning
Prevent me from sleep, and then sunlight

Conspiring in whispers against the darkness
Of cupboards, and turning impossible
Corners to spread the word to a new red

Pencil, or the fine lace pattern overhanging
The table. Only on summer afternoons,
When I prop the window open—just enough

To let the street-talk in—with an old
Library book that's long overdue, and you
Come to tea, is the silence distinct.

THE TALISMAN

There are days
I have only to open my eyes

To see the world
As bedlam, and I am in it.

Blink, and it comes
Down again to the street I live in:

There's the clatter
Of bottles on stone, and the measured

Intimate silence
Into which letters should fall—

Then footsteps
Of neighbours, patient or quick,

Who emerge
And are lost in the traffic.

Are we happy
To be here? I examine in the mirror

My naked self;
Then kiss you twice over, on the lids

Of both eyes: not
To deceive the world, or be deceived.

THE SWIMMING POOL

'It's possible,' you say, pacing the length
Of the supposed swimming pool
In our cramped back yard. Honeysuckle
Throttles the roses, but who am I
To ask for realism?—abettor
Of your ambitions, dreamer myself
Of the cottage by the sea and having
No living to earn (but I want above all
To be surprised: never to say
I had expected this).

      It becomes clear,
Doing the sums, what we are talking about
Is a true suburban dream, not wealth
Or made-to-order pools but the element
Of water, that as we stagger
Across the stepping-stones will always
Be around: something to dip into
And out of, clear and pure as nothing
We can own, as a poem in Russian that remains
Itself, however faithfully translated.

BED AND BREAKFAST

The weather affects you in certain ways
You won't or can't define: the raw, unshapely clouds
Heading nowhere in particular are clouds
After all, indistinguishable from themselves.

The sea is locked away. 'Absentee landlord' I attempt
To joke, but the situation is not funny at all,
The whole front is a sequence of lovers in cars
Whose windscreen wipers say no, repeatedly.

We are sitting on the rocks with our bottle of supermarket
     wine,
Still arguing about the wallpaper, the bidet, whether the
     curtains
Will open on the first act of a Verdi opera
Or a clear blue sky, equally impossible.

The sun, as usual, has the last word,
Dropping gently and slowly below the belt.
It teaches us nothing, but would be warmer I think
If we learned to be more tolerant of ourselves.

FEWSTON, FULL FATHOM FIVE

Once they drowned a whole village
To make a reservoir, drinking water for Leeds
That was itself overflowing . . . I imagined
The villagers of course (the real ones
Had been rehoused) swimming the streets
With torches, like cautious fish: so deep
It was always dark, but they still kept
Regular hours, emerging each morning
To buy food, newspapers, and again at night
To walk their dogs. In dry summers
You could see the tip of the church spire,
Where seagulls perched—otherwise a lake
Like any lake, indifferent to every claim
Except weather. And on warm nights
Lovers would drive from Leeds to watch
How its surface thrilled to the moon, even
To the cars' headlights on the opposite shore
That danced towards them, as in the songs.

THE DRIFTING HOUSE

Early mornings, the mist
White shadow over all, hearing
A gull's cry and the secret lap, suck, thirst
Of the unseen lake—till the house
Came clean upon me, that high black house
Built on the lakeshore by forgotten wealth,
Still standing past its prime. I watched,
Often uncertain in the widening scape
Who's watching who, whose movement
Scared the gulls; and then turned back
Towards the road I'd left.

Attempting that shore, imagining again
My morning walks, the house recedes
As backdrop to the scene: the blue sky
And the silver lake, bright birds among the trees,
And women strolling in and out
Through doors I never entered.

A VISIT TO THE BIG HOUSE

The world is either round
Like a goldfish bowl, or wide and flat
As a grand four-poster (itself a miniature
Elizabethan theatre).

I imagine making love
In such a bed: here heaven's
Within arm's reach, and behind all that,
Beyond the grinning cupids, my ancestors
Stare down in expectation of an heir.

The goldfish, meanwhile,
Are mouthing silent platitudes
In ornamental pools, the horizon blurs
With approaching rain and the final tourists
Scatter across the terrace in plastic macs.

Later, in the small hours,
When the full-length mirrors reflect each other
Across empty rooms, the doorknobs gleam
Like skulls in their submarine kingdom.

FREEHOLD

Now the house is empty. But we are here
To listen in to our own perceptions
And string them together down the damp, badly lit corridor
That leads, if anywhere, to a door that's locked.

Magazines in piles, a mattress, golf club, an alarm clock
In working order they must have left by mistake
Yield an identikit portrait
Of who lived here, what they liked and did, but not

Truly who they were: that girl in a pink dress
Among the greys and greens of the yard outside, turning
And turning just one more page
Before she comes indoors, is she happy? Not? Does the
    book

End well? Our questions grate on silence, an endlessly
Receding mirror that gives us back ourselves, again
And again: muffled echoes, the gods
Complaining about the terms of their lease.

THE COLLECTOR

Small change
Falls from his hand, tinkling down there
As if his fingers had riffled
The keys of an old piano.

Distracted
By his own name, called by a woman
Who must want him to catch a train or something,
He leaves a cigar burning

And a foreign
Newspaper. The headlines don't bear reading,
Nor the columns of stock-exchange closing prices
He's ringed with haloes,

But the coins—
A tip, *pourboire*—race in the mind
Like a tune you can't get rid of,
Long after the words have been forgotten.

So he departs
Towards a moment of welcome or parting
The song includes. And somewhere out there
He becomes its theme: framed

By the vast
Neo-Classical arches, he explores the necessity
Of the first encounter—sudden fusion of eyes
Across the milling, madding crowd

That stops
The blood, that's charged with the promise
Of understanding—or the long last kiss
That proves as finite as the others.

    Some of these moments
People are carrying around, testing
Against the new world: discarding, exchanging
At market rates. And some are hoarded

    In attics,
In boudoirs of the house too intimate
To enter, collector's pieces sold as a lot
By the collector's heirs, to pay off debts.

HOUSE OF CARDS

Ah there, there on the headland
Is our fisherman's shack knocked together from planks and
    things
We have no other use for, there can be
No other use. Open to all weathers, vapours,
Doldrums of the spirit, shrouded for months on end in a
    mist
Nothing can penetrate, no messages get through, nothing
To comfort or bring relief—how even a tree
Can survive there, frayed and reckless and utterly bare,
Offering no shade, no fruit worth eating, how it draws its
    sap
From stone, is a mystery past knowing. But it does;
And sometimes there's an ageless, nameless couple there
Who eat pickles by the jar and salted herring,
Continually repaint the walls to match our restlessness,
Play bezique all night with our diminishing pack of cards
Until they've lost them all and there's nothing left for
    anyone to do
But wait for the sun to come out. No wonder they say

I could go mad in a place like that—besides,
What do I know about fishing? Only the lure
Of its skills: patience and cunning; the arcane lore
Of tackle and rod, unravelling knots in the tangled net;
The practice of solitude and the sly kinship with fish
That grows in the blood, like desire—a sweetness,
A spreading warmth—urgent as evolution
On this bleak, eroded headland where the wind, and the sea
Tumbling on rocks, never hesitate one moment.

TREES, FOR EXAMPLE

Trees about the house, filtering the glare
To a tolerable shade, locking the house to the hillside
With their own roots—where you lay
And daydreamed all morning of foreign countries.

Now scrambling the light
On their summer green, burgeoning
With spontaneous applause; now winter-bare,
Scratched on the sky by the hand, say,

Of a long-term prisoner who no longer sees the point
Of marking off days with neat, vertical strokes
Around and around his cell.
And now it's the trees you dream of

But different to how you remember them,
A measure of what you've become:
Mile upon mile of rocky coastline, and trees
Bent double by the prevailing wind.

EXILE

We have been drinking all morning.
The barman claims he knew my father
Which is impossible, but I take some comfort in it.

The map curls on the opposite wall,
Already out of date when the war began,
And three soldiers slumped in the corner

Are watching my every move,
As if just waiting to be given the sign.
I could walk straight out of this smoke-filled bar

But somewhere on the map—
And I'm still trying to find exactly where—
There's a village beside a river,

Trees bolt upright in the cloudless sky,
And one dark room in which a child's finger
Has also stopped the spinning globe.

A SMALL TOWN ON THE COAST

The youngest son who made it to the city
Stays in the city. His twin passions are for music
And mathematics: horizontals of roofs, gutters,
The vertical streetlamp tapering to a curve,
And the continuous whispering graze of traffic
Late at night—unmistakably the sea, the sea
That mocked him even then, daring him to cross it.

Some girls can be impressed by his talk of that,
Daybreak and a clean world. Now on winter Sundays
His bed's the only warm place, where he remembers
Schoolmates, cousins, the faces passing and repassing
In the cobbled square. His mother still writes, boasting
Of his sister's seven children and Space Invaders
In the new arcade that used to be the baker's.

DESERT REST HOUSE

A radio bleats, a dog
Ponders a rat, clawed and half-alive—
This is nowhere, nothing, a one-night stand
Anonymous, available.

Gradations of colour and shadow
Presage no angels, we watch them
For what they are, symptoms of a disease
At large within us.

A wrecked car is being explored
By children—as ours will be,
Though the mechanic swears
It's fixed now, we can go on.

The light curdles on walls.
Tracks lead off, ruts,
Into that brief cold clarity
Preceding night, or dawn.

THE ARABIAN BIRD

> *. . . forty days journey; and in all this way there is scarce any*
> *green thing to be met with, nor beast nor fowl to be seen or*
> *heard; nothing but sand and stones, excepting one place which*
> *we passed through by night; I suppose it was a village, where*
> *were some trees, and, we thought, gardens.*
> —The Pilgrimage of Joseph Pitts to Meccah and Medina, 1680

Blistered and parched, days past count
we had travelled since then: I remembered
nothing, there was nothing to remember here
or feel, a tomb it was and the sun
bled us dry and blind as the stones.

Until that night, hearing a sound
as of men talking in the other room,
I catch a voice but not its words

But this not a voice, though a shrill
trembling of the black acacias
spoke then of gardens,
a green-tiled town, and of the lap of water
in the fountain court, like lips I've known.

Then the wound opened, bled freely
and a startled bird took flight.
I felt the heat and the gust of its wing.

STORKS

Before or after, the condition of heaven.
We spoke our memories and our hopes,
Elaborate shadows not wholly believed in
Except to prove the substance of the moment.

And the place itself mock-paradise,
The Chellah gardens in early summer
Fed by a whole dead dynasty of kings.
Now the barbarians have come and gone
The looted necropolis reverts to nature
But nature changed, manhandled,
Human in its entanglements, its profusions
Of reds and yellows against the deeper green:
A child's favourites, to be freely picked.

A stork's makeshift nest
Overhung the stump of a ruined minaret.
The female bird stood awkwardly one-legged,
Ungainly and unafraid, preening
And scratching with her impeccable beak—
Vanity, vanity, amusing in others—
Her majesty mocked by her gift to mimic,
Most ridiculous when most human,
Most elegant in flight.

Earnest sparrows flashed to and fro
And from the river came her mate,
So gorged on fish he must have charmed the air.

He wheeled above, a last free dalliance
Before the plunge to earth;
She clacked and gibbered, tossed head to wings
So her whole soft under-neck was bared.

His landing at last seemed hit-or-miss,
An act of faith—the wings failing,
The splayed feet grappling wildly for a hold—
A lifetime's practice has not cut the risk.

CAIRO NIGHT-CLUB

As the voices slur her accent comes distinct
The Texan heiress with the Lebanese, the exiled rich.
We are watching dwarves and juggling children,
A dancer's thighs in the harsh red light, and when
The girls are bought and our company half-gone
A boy comes on, he's pale as dawn, flashing his body
To her heavy eyes—Veronique, ageing and blonde,
Declines into sleep, a temporary refuge.

For the war goes on, we take it for granted,
We all have our dead. The Lebanese jockey,
The small, aggressive one, says at the Beirut racetrack
The horses went berserk. 'They ran around,
Bashing their heads against trees, killing themselves.'

1977

I REMEMBER

A fat Greek was throwing plates
On the floor, one by one; when a sea-wind
Swept through the door—and a girl
At her most extreme and on her own
Saying yes to solve uncertainty.

Nothing fixed or permanent,
Things caught on the wing and lost as quick:
For the past dies off thank God, shrivels
And falls or is cut at will, only a few
Close-knotted roots will not come out.

ROXY SQUARE

The ice cream melts on her tongue.
Unchaperoned at last, she smiles
At the young policeman in his hopeless
Mess with traffic, the cars and carts
And donkeys braying bedlam.

Businessmen in the café look up
From conversation, from their table
Falls a shower of crumbs and the cats
Scramble—as his whistle shrills
At a bike that's jumped the kerb.

The rider brakes, adjusts his mirror
To catch her motion through the evening
Crowd: the dust and wrappings crackle
At her feet, the spring flamboyant
Breaks fire-sheets on her shoulder.

SHY MOUNTAIN CHILDREN

One, another, then two more appear
And disappear behind the rocks—it's their flash
And sparkle gives them away, the sudden shine
Of eyes and teeth and flowing hair, as they flit
Like birds beside the path.

They must have followed us
From the village we had passed,
The few bare, scrubbed huts of mud and straw
Still as the Sabbath and nobody there
But one woman clothed in red who stared at us
From an open loft. Suppose, I thought,
Suppose I had been born . . .

We stopped at the river and watched them come:
Small, dark, alert to every sign.
One girl was boldest, gripping your scarf
And not letting go, then touching your hair
With her tiny hands. One boy stood back
And pulled a face, as if afraid
We'd vanish if he smiled, or of our want
To give them something better than we had.

She took your scarf of course, the girl
The others followed, running barefoot
Back the way we'd come. And we waded
Across the shallow river and climbed the bank
To the hot, new-surfaced road. Refreshed
And exhausted by the high bright air

We fell asleep in the local bus.
I dreamt I was at home, but there was water
Brilliant and cold, and children running there—
Then woke to foreign voices
And the lights of an unknown town.

TABLE TALK

He was blind you said, I doubted that.
Everywhere he found us out, in every bar
And café in the town—grinning, leaning idly
On his crutches, parading his stumps
In mockery of our legs. Our conversation froze.

I dropped him coins: he'd mumble as they fell
And kiss the ground, and then look up
And stare straight through us—at the fly perhaps
On the plastic flowers, or at some vague,
Contextual heaven we couldn't enter.

At last, about to start on our umpteenth stew
Of native beans, you said 'No, I wouldn't want
To *live* here'—and he rose and heaped our plates
With rare delicacies, promising
That nowhere else we'd taste the like.

NEWLY MARRIEDS IN THE SECOND-HAND COOKERY SECTION

I lower my eyes
To evade the bookseller, as if he were the priest
And I a tourist, a pagan voyeur
Of books that I don't believe in.

Immaculate confections and remedies for gout,
What have these to do with us?
With your painter's instinct for colour and risk?

All the fatal, forbidden fruits
Lie mouldering on the shelves, tempting
The worms only; nor is it book-knowledge,
Knowing when to say *when*.

But here, oh here is our Egyptian dish,
Disguised in print—here are the flies,
The heat, and the carcasses
Strung from the trees like melting wax.

We ate that night till bloated,
Then staggered home and couldn't sleep.
Tomorrow, we said, we shall be stricter—

Today, tasting nostalgia like a quaint
Aphrodisiac, we carry the book
To the dotty old bookseller
Who takes us for adults, who can come to no harm.

LOCAL GOSSIP

Where were we? In the café
In Heliopolis, sunning ourselves
In the neo-colonial climate
Of a country where even the poorest
Had a smile for our camera?
Or dining late in the local Indian,
With our coats and scarves still on
Against the draught of London winter
The door let in? On the table
Your notebook and glasses, I am
Truly amazed by their patient
Forbearance of all our silences
And gossip. Wherever it was
We were far too tired, neither awake
Nor aware enough to notice
The time and place. What I remember
Is asking what they had to eat
And the waiter's shrug, a gesture
Suggesting a kind of freedom
That might, after all, be just that.

AFTERNOON IN NAPLES

We climbed up
Through narrow, overhanging streets
That the sun couldn't reach,
Distracted by cooking smells

And rooms we had no access to,
Cluttered with wardrobes
And giant beds, framed madonnas
And the photographs of absent relatives.

Even high up, where the rich lived
And dressed more like us, where the map
Promised gardens and open spaces,
The streets abruptly turned

And blocked the view, the famous view
With everything in it, the bay
And the dead volcano and the houses
Crowding the slopes, dazzling on postcards.

We came down at last
To the man who sold shellfish
From a seaside cart, with wooden sticks
To prise them out.

His little yellow light-bulbs
Bobbed up and down
Against the wide, soft, horizontal of the sea
Like pinpricks in the dark.

CHINESE PUPPETS

The light was bad,
I had to bend to their glass-covered case
    To see where the strings
Were attached, that made them dance—
    Fine, delicate threads,
Visible only to the naked eye.
    We were watched
By hollow, almost life-sized dummies
    In rusted armour,
Watching ourselves in the glass.
    The rain was falling
To meet itself in the Grand Canal,
    Even the eels
In the fish-market, captured in boxes,
    Echoed exactly
Another time, when you walked barefoot
    On the sunlit deck
And watched the same eels slowly dying.
    You called me
To see them, across the wet piazza—
    Ah Venice, Venice,
Who is the fairest of them all?

JOACHIM'S DREAM

High on the wall an angel
Flies, above a landscape
Of rocks, bushes, and the wooden hut
Of a sleeping saint.

He is watched by two reverent
Peasants, and a party of German
Schoolchildren. Their teacher
Is shouting, explaining everything.

Sitting in the café outside,
Waiting for the sun to come through,
I write on the postcard how fine
It all is, how worthwhile

My coming here. In the chapel,
Closed now to tourists and the lights
Switched off, the sky
Is cracked, blistered, forever blue.

LE PROFESSEUR CIVILISĒ

The boy, woken by moonlight,
Stands at the window, watched
From the doorway by a learned
Childless man.

The picture's almost still
Except that the boy
Is gently rocking on his feet.
The moon's light

Defines them both:
Itard, who gave what love
A man can give, and the boy
He named Victor.

WHITE RUSSIAN

Write him down you said, the old
French gentleman we met in Paris,
The one with the labrador dog
And the dead White Russian wife.

She painted blood-red flowers
And pallid women with slender necks,
Memorials to a remote childhood
That history had gobbled.

They hung like ikons in his room,
Very cold and still. We sat
In their shadows, at a table
Laid with ancient bread and cheese,

While he spoke of Anna Semonovna,
And of driving down to Cannes
In a white Rolls Royce. Before long
You wanted to escape that place,

His room with its curtains drawn
Against the little daylight left,
So we hurriedly wrote addresses
And were free to go. The darkness

Oppressed you, made darker still
By the quickness of his mind,
And an hour later in the galleries
Of the outdated Musée de l'Art Moderne

It still persisted. Remember
I love you, remember it was he,
As we crossed the street from the café,
Who placed himself in our hands.

THE WASP AT GIDEAU'S COTTAGE

The barn's door is a round black mouth
Saying nothing, nothing at all
To this dreamy day. Spreadeagled
On the grass, we might as well be birds

Or fishes swimming through the lavish field,
Easy in their element, except the wasp
Has found you out: it nags and nags
Insistently, as if attempting to complete

Some half-remembered line, and you turn
On your side and ask: 'That crazy
Half-starved man in there who's lying
In his filth—do I imagine him?'

TRAVELLING BACK

In a poor country, there's joy
In mere survival—arriving late, finding a room
For the night, children everywhere.

You could buy them by the hour—
But not the women, who were veiled or absent.
The man nodded, prepared to bargain.

One watched me as I ate, not for money
But to lick the empty bowl when I let it go.
I, in turn, watched him, his village

Of corrugated iron and mud-brick houses
Stitched to the hillside, its single winding street
Like a nursery rhyme I knew by heart.

44

PICTURE POSTCARDS

1 *Ex-colonial*

Send them to lovers and favourite aunts
Wishing you were here

But keep one
To remind you of what it was not like

Glittering white facades
Hard-edged as in dreams, the sky

Cloudless, the sea too blue
To be true, an old limousine or two

Cruising along Marine Drive
With all the time in the world

2 *Red Square, 1913*

Those smudges in the background
(Not the furry black holes

Arranged in rows along the walls)
Are the beginnings of crowds

Meanwhile, nothing could be clearer
Against the blanket of snow

Than the face of this teenage princess
Too bored even to pose

And a child in mansize cap and boots
Staring back at the photographer

3 *Uranus*

Waiting for history to arrive
As it were, on one's doorstep

One is constantly referring back
To the early SF comics

And children's encyclopaedias,
One is trying it seems

To remember what happened
Pre-natally, when I was only a gleam

In my father's eye: everything here
Being unexpectedly familiar

4 *Harrogate*

How, she asked,
Do they get the colours in the right places?

My grandmother gripping one postcard
In her trembling hand, resistant

To knitting & gossip & television
And the mild, appeasing smiles

Of unrecognized visitors who come and go
Through the hotel lounge: my grandmother

There in her chair, *her* chair
By the window, the window marked X

HERE AND THERE

There, you took all men's eyes
And women's too, all they
And the children running to snatch your dress
Played bit-parts in your pageant.

Sunlight fired you, and from
Your rapid, random talk that struggled
To keep pace with your excitement,
I caught the word 'free . . .'

Too many beggars
Made me slow to assent, or my thoughts
Of returning home, or of how close
And bare the desert was.

Now in November you are walking
In the early dark along North End Road,
And I see you again in the colour
And squalor of that hot bazaar.

Scuffing through leaves and the fruit
Fallen from the empty stalls . . .

Dark figures swarm behind you
As you come towards me, smiling.

TALK ABOUT THE WEATHER

Days the sea and the sky don't bother
To define themselves, but meet in a tremulous blur
That could be either. Still half-asleep, you get up
To a morning of padding about in slippers,
An indoors existence: how like the English, you say,
To be good at watercolours, sketchbook variations
On the seasonal stereotypes—autumn is a pale,
Yellowish wash the land soaks into, spring
A cluster of migrant birds on the telephone wires
Like notes in a classical score . . . Even their poems
Are neat, suburban gardens whose hybrid roses
Repeat themselves year after year, and scratch
Your hand with their dry thorns. The civil war
Is ranked as a history-book episode—no blood,
Yet, on our doorstep—but the odds are lengthening
On the kind of summer that should be everyone's
Birthright, you worry about the plants and these
Are the tricky days, when both or one of us
Is bound to wish we were somewhere else.

MORNING POEM

Now is sunlight on our table
On coffee cooling in chipped blue mugs,
Your hair too and your eyes reflect
This invasion of light.

You are a child in Italy
Breakfasting with your father I'll never meet,
While slowly across the lake
The night fishing boats return.

LILLIE ROAD, JANUARY 3rd

'Nowt wrong with happiness'—
Big red nose and watery eyes
And a suit fit for a wedding,
Seeing us dance at the bus stop.

Then he in The Traveller's Rest
And we feeling the cold. That day,
The first you wore them, you lost
One ear-ring—there? Still? Washed

In the gutter, under the crumpled
Silver foil from a packet of cigarettes?
You said, 'You must stop smoking.'
I pretended not to hear

But the ghosts heard, looking out
Through broken black windows
From abandoned homes. 'So many
Junk shops here, who buys this stuff?'

Then a 74 bus, *deus ex machina*.

(The first Sunday
Of a new year, and your birthday.)

Empty street, glad ghosts.

PONTEFRACT CASTLE

'Every childhood is provincial . . .'

The day before, they had found six skeletons,
Two of them sitting up: was it by accident,
How the bodies just happened to fall
Into the pit, or by design? Perhaps those
Buried sitting could never enter Heaven.

The stench from the glue factory drove us
Inside the caravan, where Mrs Heaton made tea.
Where's Alice? she asked. And the man
From the university, who'd promised to be there?
Smiling, superior, she told us how glue was made

From dead pigs; also how, at the weekend,
A woman was raped in a nearby street—
Right there, in the *Evening Post*, her finger
Jabbing the print, the windows steaming up
With our hot close breath, the kettle screaming.

I walked the girl to the bus station, both of us
Returning to Leeds. We sat upright, stilted,
Thigh by cooling thigh; in my pocket
A piece of broken china, patterned exactly
Like my grandmother's chipped plates.

SALOME

Problems of state,
Problems with wives, daughters, as if the mere
Juxtaposition of a breakfast quarrel and, say,
The invasion of Afghanistan were itself significant.

My attention drifts
To the green-eyed girl beneath the exit lights
Who is filing her nails, oblivious
To the prisoner's loud, astounding prophecies.

Yet to kill him now
Would make a dangerous martyr: already
There are knives, rumours, illegible graffiti
On the tenement walls, already you suspect

That the lone rider
Descending the valley, hooves clattering now
Through the torch-lit gateway, will arrive
Just a moment too late to make any difference.

And when the fat king
Tells the dancing girl she can have anything she wants,
Anything in the world, you suddenly realize
That he, at least, has been doomed from the start.

THE HUNT

For days after, the stars at night
Were the beast's eyes. Its blood poured
From the hole I must have made.

This was not my intention. The day
Had begun well, back there in the sunlit
Clearing among the riders in costume

And the dogs yelping, bounding all over
With eager impatience and covering
My face with their hot tongues.

Now the sky has healed and I go about
With my head high, bending an ear
To the silent forest. I cannot say

It was an accident. The hawk
Weighs on my fist, and the small
White flowers are trampled underfoot.

THE GREEN MAN

Somewhere in the forest
I lost my way, if ever
I had one. I doubt that
Now, but then it was clear
As my face in the pool
I was remembered somewhere
And somewhere expected
And whose was the way
If not my own? For hours
I stumbled about, dark
Must have fallen but still
The frogs kept on calling
My name and the animals
Growled in their thickets,
Birds chirruped and twittered
And flashed between branches
Too quick for the eye, I
Struggled to reach them but
The trees, even the trees
Became shadows that danced
And fled, oh fled from me
And I ran and gripped one
Silly leaf and pressed it
In my fist. Now my palm
Is green, now the green man
Has woken from his dream.

DESK OBJECT

They tremble in his presence
On silver stems, teasing his need
To get a hold on life
And make them still.

They are black
Balloons, or toffee apples,
Or heads on spikes, medieval
Deterrents: this,

They declare, is justice—
Not the Mercator projection
He seems to inhabit,
But the true

And passing record of every breath,
Gathered and lost
On their surface shine. Like eyes
Glued open, and perhaps

Hollow after all, they are ugly,
Useless, and cannot
Be ignored: they strain the nerve
That makes him blink.

THE LONDON UNDERGROUND

How can you bear it, the continuous
Artificial light? The layers of make-up
On unwashed cheeks, eyes still gummy with sleep,
Lips mouthing headlines across your shoulder?

Or such a casual, heart-felt intimacy
As a girl burying her face
In a child's neck, the least expected thing?

Suddenly, there is nowhere to look.

ADDRESSING THE LADY

No one of that name lives here. I don't know,
I haven't been here long . . . But the name
Is not wrong, nor is the house, a good house
That wears its pretensions lightly
As if it knows they are only superficial.
(Lodgers? I hear the lady thinking:
You must be thinking of another street.)

Still, we agree they are worth keeping up:
Chiselled window gables, miniature buttresses
Beneath a roof that has no need to overhang
But does so, for their sake. They are a kind
Of tribute to the few trees that remain
And share with these (but not the lady,
Who frankly suspects I know more than I should)

A gently weathered look, an air of grace
That is not put out by dogshit, municipal
Lamp-posts or the apple that gapes, half eaten,
On the pavement between us. For a moment
I am tempted to stay, to coax from this woman
Through the infinite solicitude of summer afternoons
And cadences of pillow talk, that secret

The house shelters—a whisper, a drifting scent
Of damp blossom, suddenly a wind
Bellying the curtains and she stares, as she closes
The door, as if I had casually mentioned
The birthmark on her thigh. So thank you, madam,
I say with respect, with increased wonder
At the form such meetings can take.

CATS

The cat I lived with once soon left me
For the neighbours—more food, more love,
Any human would have done the same.

I watch it now grow fat and sleek,
And how it sniffs the air before it leaps
As if measuring what's to be gained.

Worldly-wise—how else be wise?
Yet what they're deified for, is their
Moody adolescence, their quick reversals

From rest to zest, from skittishness
To stealth, shameless betrayals and cries
Of love that wake me in the night.

A SHORTER BESTIARY

Cuttlefish

It is just possible
That the only other man in the bar
Has devoted his entire life to the study
Of cuttlefish, a queer fish

That seems specifically designed
To get under the skin of things.

I shall ask him what they eat
And how to tell the females from the males, etc.
One has got, after all, to begin somewhere.

Owl

The late bird catches the early mouse,
And other such gobbets.
                           Old bleary-eyes,
Droopy-head, perched up there
Like an uncle after lunch, he knows you know
There's little worth saying that can't be said
With a nod and a wink.

Giraffe

You would think
With that long neck of his that he,
If anyone, could get what he wants.

But somehow the tastiest leaves
Are always too high, or round corners,
Or another giraffe has got there first.

One of these days he'll wake up early
And strip that tree to its bare bones.

THE FARMER'S WIFE

Are the fences secure? And the water tank,
The rusted old bath in the farthest field,
Not leaking? The farmer is thinking
Was he a fool to hire this thin town boy
Who watches him now as he eats.

Man and boy disappear in the mist
Towards the sound of cows. Without milking,
Their udders would swell like vast balloons,
The grass rise to the height of trees
And swallow the house utterly.

In the kitchen, a woman is placing
Eggs in cardboard trays. They are piled high
In a china bowl, still warm from the hen-house,
Each one to be picked and cleaned
And placed with care, while the men are out.

STRANGER ON A TRAIN

The writing on the window
Is riddled with clichés, a 'realistic' landscape
For the stranger killing time.

Here's the train
Chuff-chuffing past the allotments
And yellow bedroom curtains of the final terrace,

Two men carrying paint
Forever across a field, the loyal station-master
Easing his feet into dog-eared slippers

And that bare, swept platform
Where I'll finally step, avoiding the puddles
And fumbling in pockets for the porter's tip.

Soon, now, this train
Will turn quietly inside out, whenever I look out
There'll be myself looking in through the glass—

That boy, up by the fence
On the embankment's edge, above the scree of tangled
Bushes, refuse and scorched grass, waving

And waving to nobody who is here.

THE CROSSING KEEPER

A depression moving southwards
Crosses the railway line at exactly the moment
The car arrives at the end of a line
Of cars, bicycles, impatient to get through.

The engine shudders to a halt
To a jangle of keys. It's all electric now,
Lights flashing and a flimsy bar
Across my half of the road: the other half leads back.

The ashtray is full to choking. Cows
Doze in the field, an abandoned combine harvester
Gathers dust till Monday: it's on days like this
I'd get hay fever, have to lie indoors

Red-eyed and puffy, while sunlight
Flickered through curtains and the air brimmed
With the voices of guests, having tea
And ice cream in the garden outside.

Their conversation drifted
Like a stray cloud, impossibly remote, their laughter
Is a butterfly skimming the poppies
In hardly a breath of wind.

And almost before you've noticed it
A sealed train has approached
Without even a whistle and is already gone.
It leaves an exaggerated silence

The old crossing keeper enters, dragging the gate
Back across the lines, then cupping
His hands to relight his pipe—
Seeing a matchbox there on the verge.

THE VILLAGER'S TALE

There was a storm once
Is unlikely to be forgotten, now the guidebooks
Elaborate with scholarly detail
The marvellous frescoes that were destroyed.

Skilled hand and visionary eye
Were one, they claim, in the execution of belief
On a bare wall: not
That we recognized that, simply the shock

Of seeing ourselves up there
As saints and demons, and they among us
Ploughing our fields, or idling on the green
By the bridge, our meeting place.

On the night of the storm I lay with Mary
In the tithe barn by the river.
She was drowned in the flood, the flood
Took everything . . . There, now, the date

And the highest level the water reached—
But she was too far out to reach,
No one could have saved her
Or that image of her, her perfect likeness—

Are marked on the wall where the youngsters sit
Kicking their heels, ogling the girls
Out of school and the tourists' foreign cars.
The barn was declared unsafe

And pulled down, also that house
Where the idiot child was locked, so long
We forgot he was there—but remember
Him often now in the silence, his quiet knocking.

PIECES OF WOOD

Not the divining fork, mere tool
Of an optimist till it comes
Across the coincidence of belief
And water, when it may dance.

Nor the mast, braving the winds
And ocean, and supporting
So much width of canvas
Upon so very little.

Nor a match of course, consumed
Like a kamikaze by the flame
It makes. But something more down
To earth, encountering small

Obstacles, testing the way
For each change of element
From stone to water, from air
To stone, as a white stick does.

FIRST FALL

Clear, cool, and unannounced, it begins
With a certain smile, like a door opening
In another town: in the blink

Of an eyelid, in the eyes
Of the girl you are watching who suddenly
Turns and catches your own: in a wave

Or the sound of waves
In the shell that you hold to your ear:
In the gossip of women coming early

To market (the mist is rising
Above the hills that surround this town)
In a voice or the tone of that voice

Clear, cool, and unannounced, it begins
With a flurry of sudden snow
That lightly drifts against my hot cheeks.